The coloring book of all shapes and forms

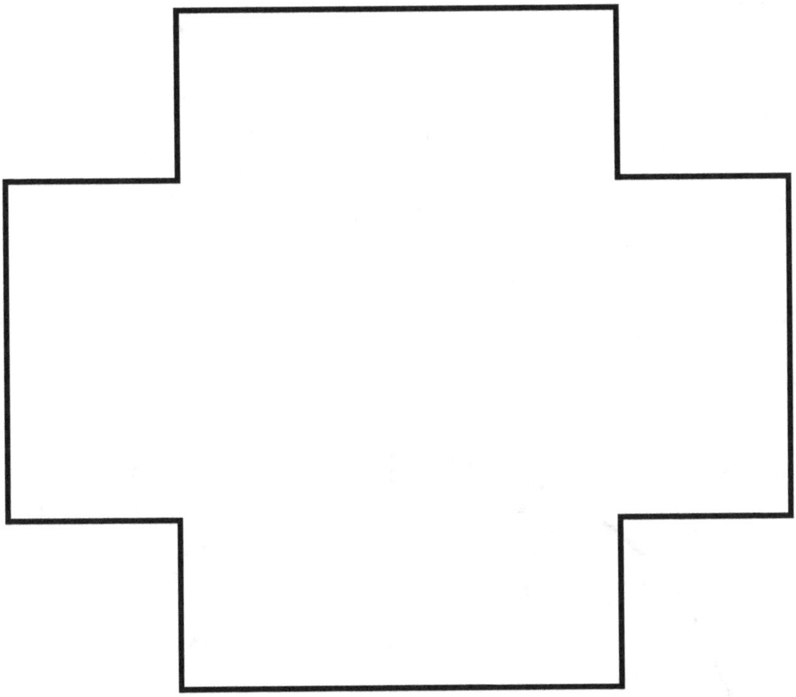

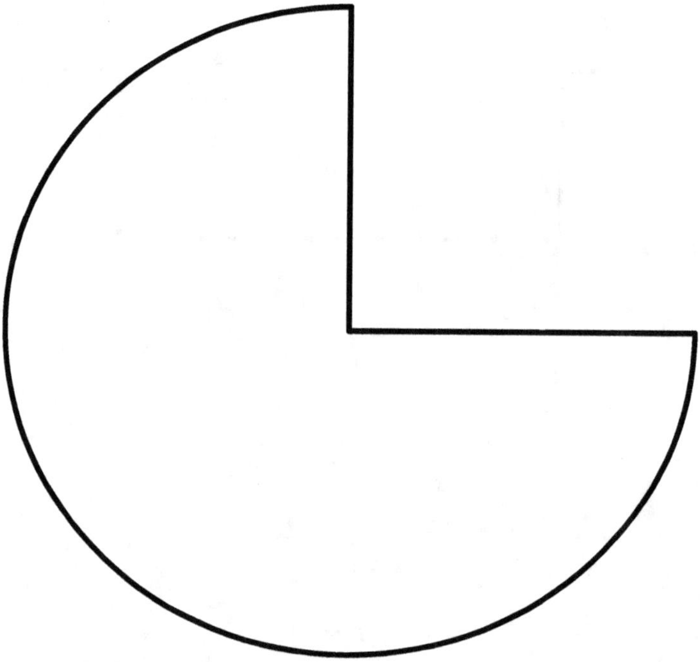

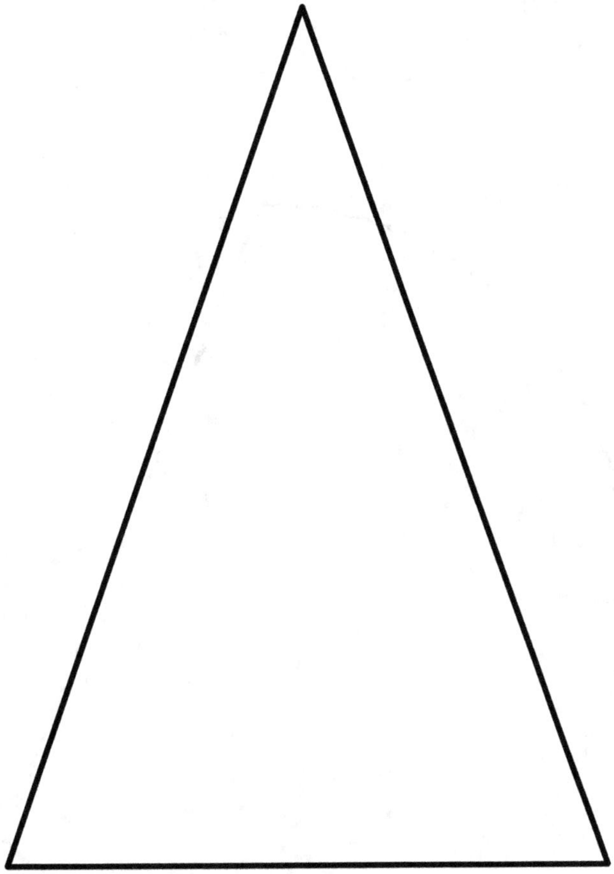

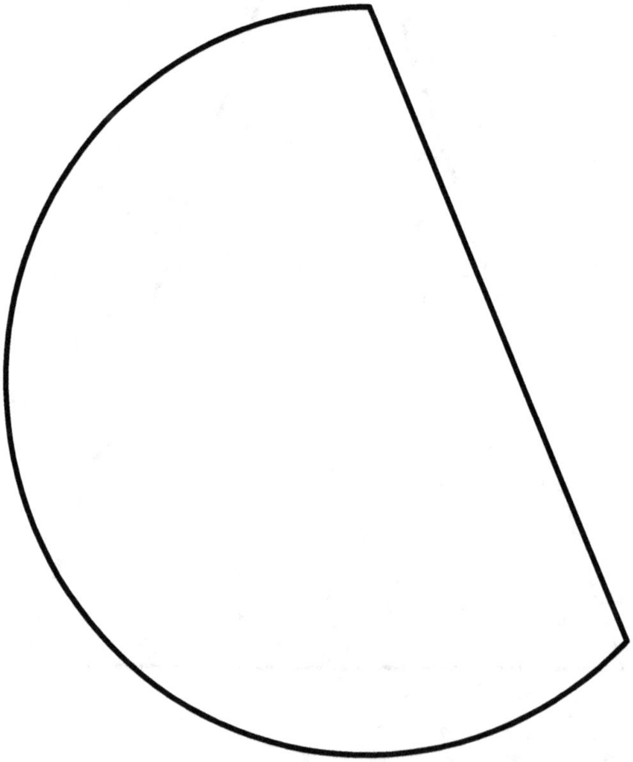

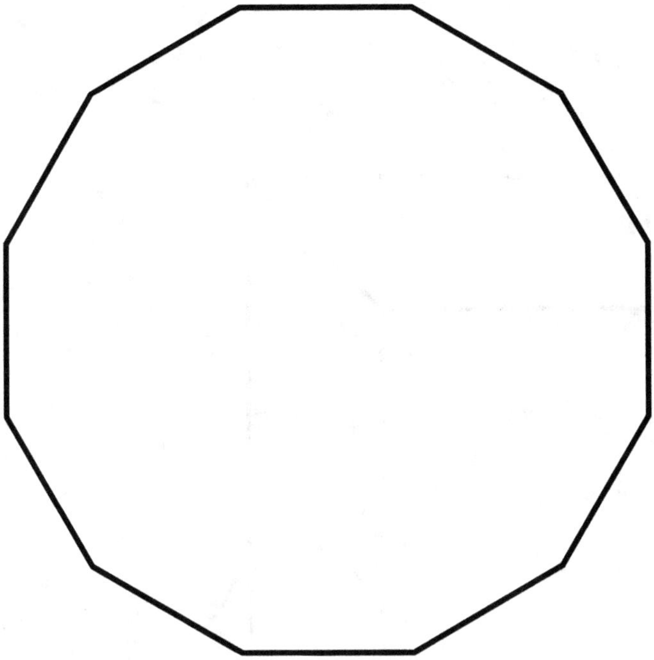

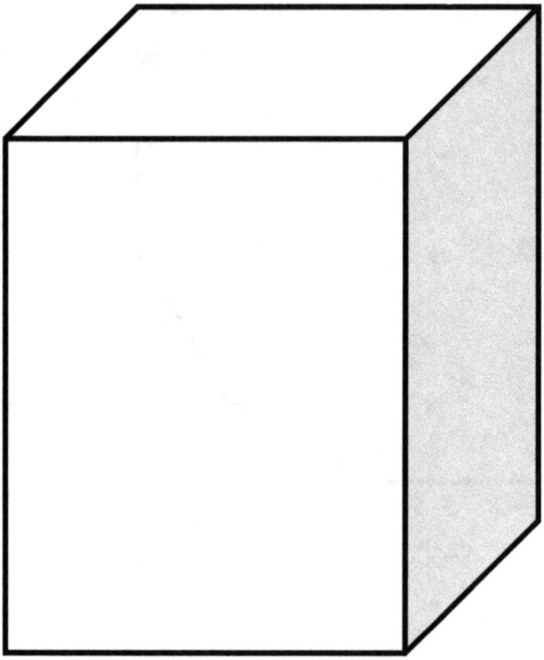

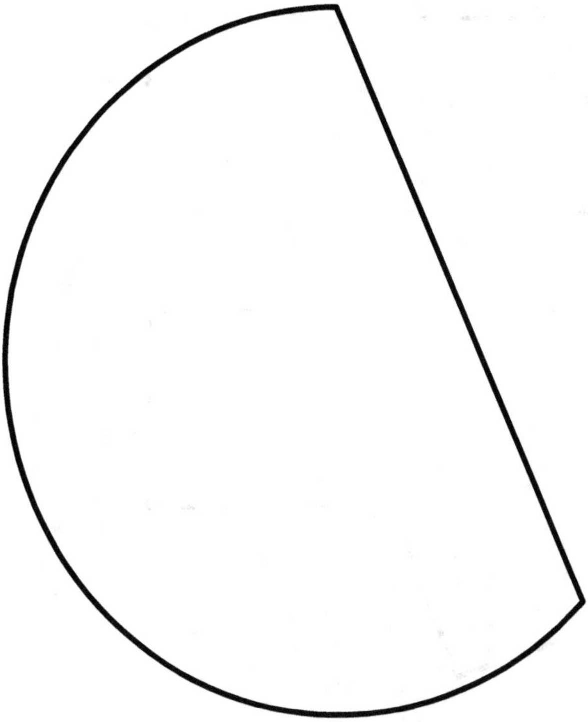

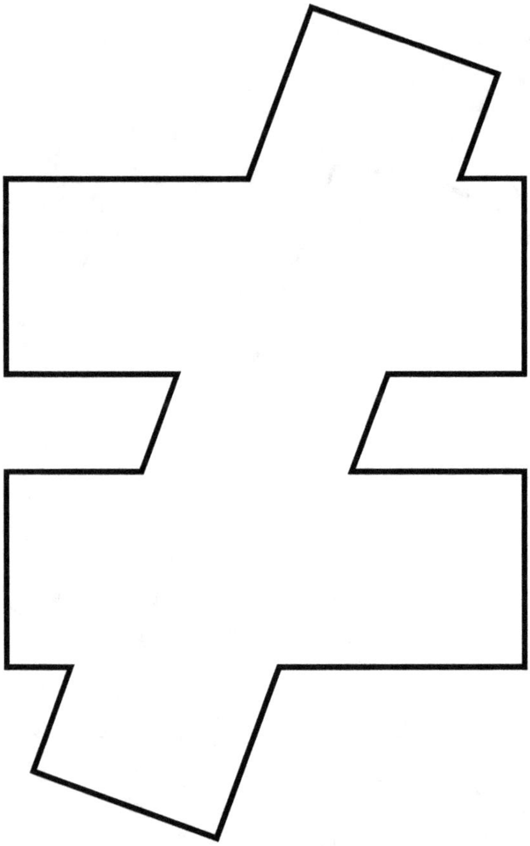

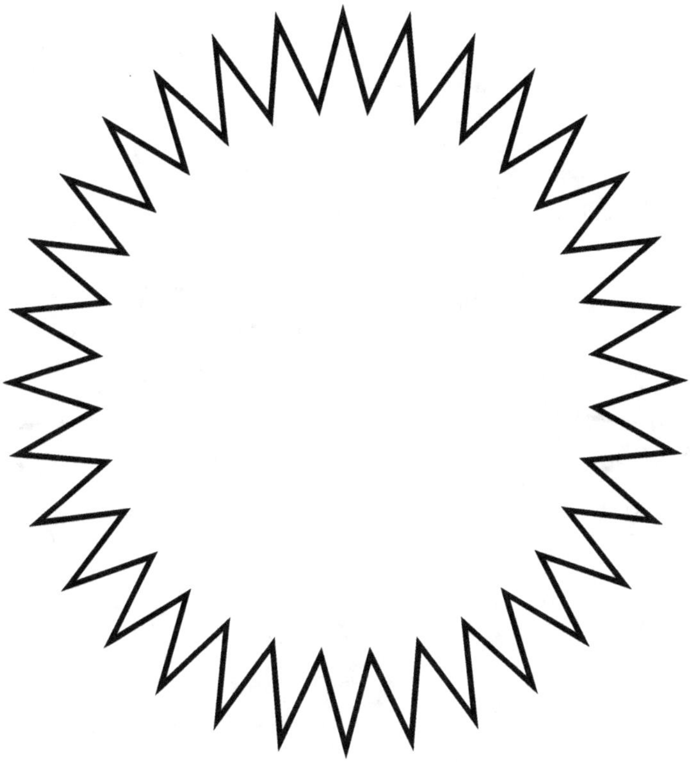

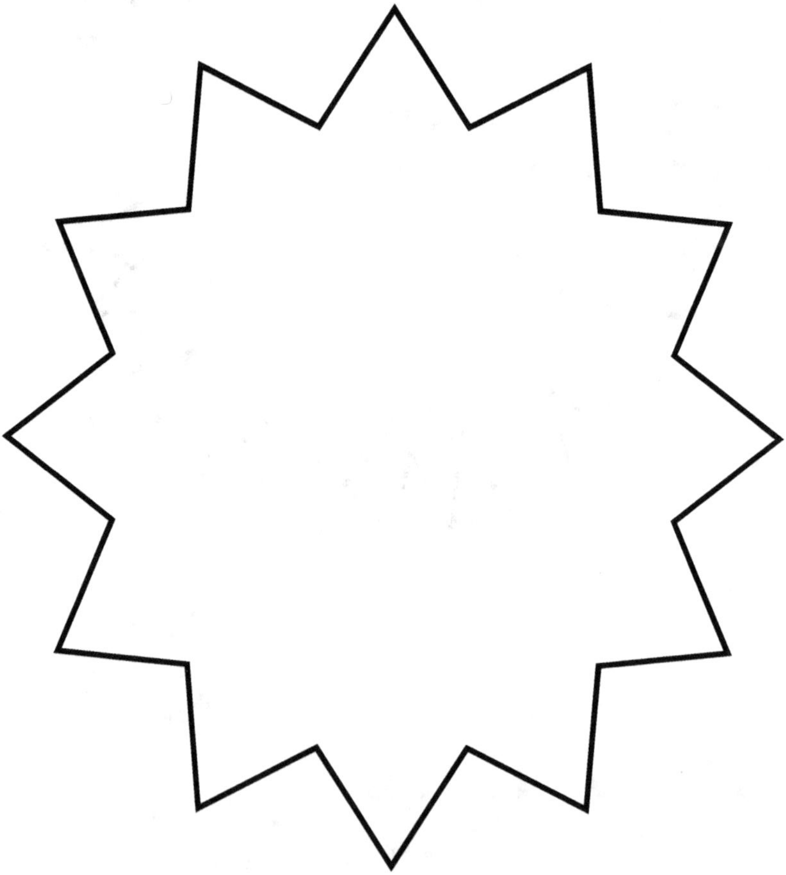

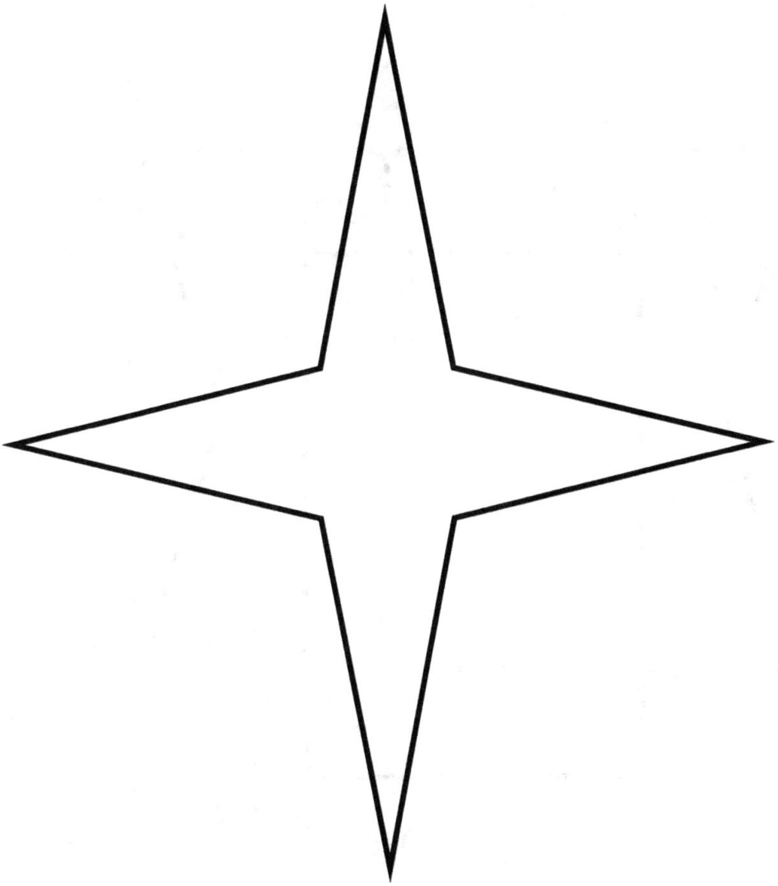

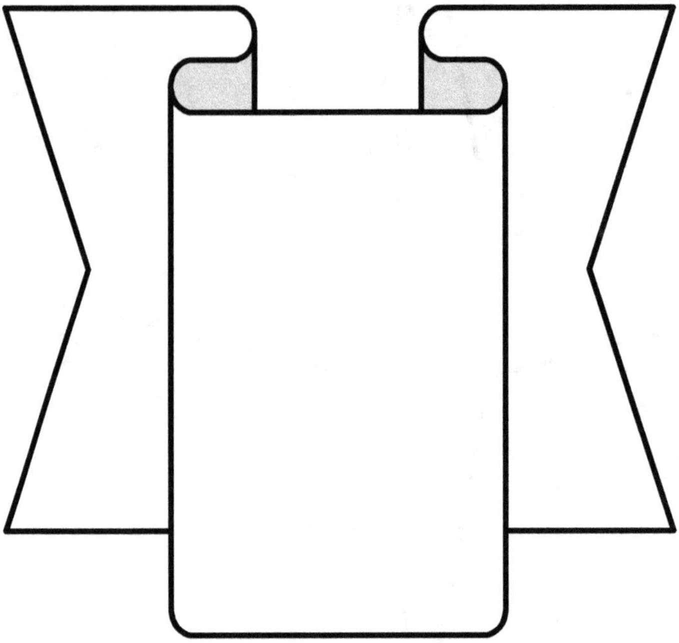

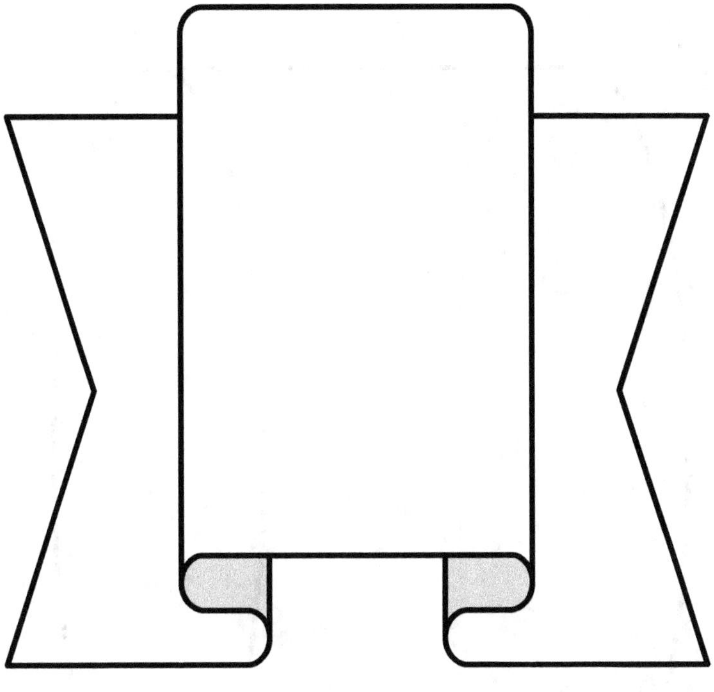

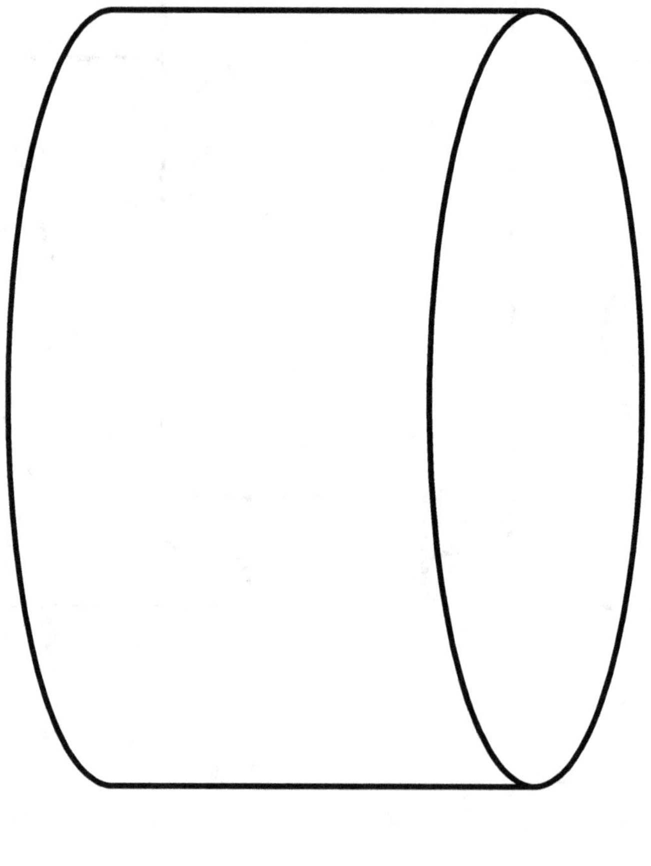

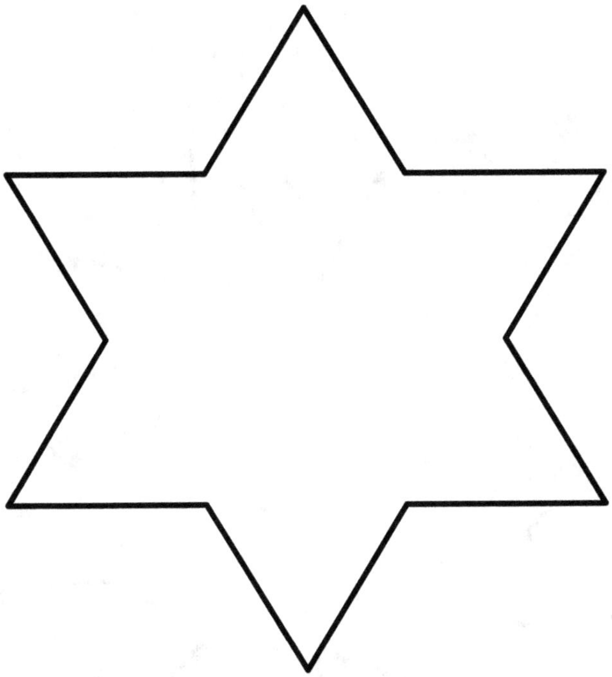

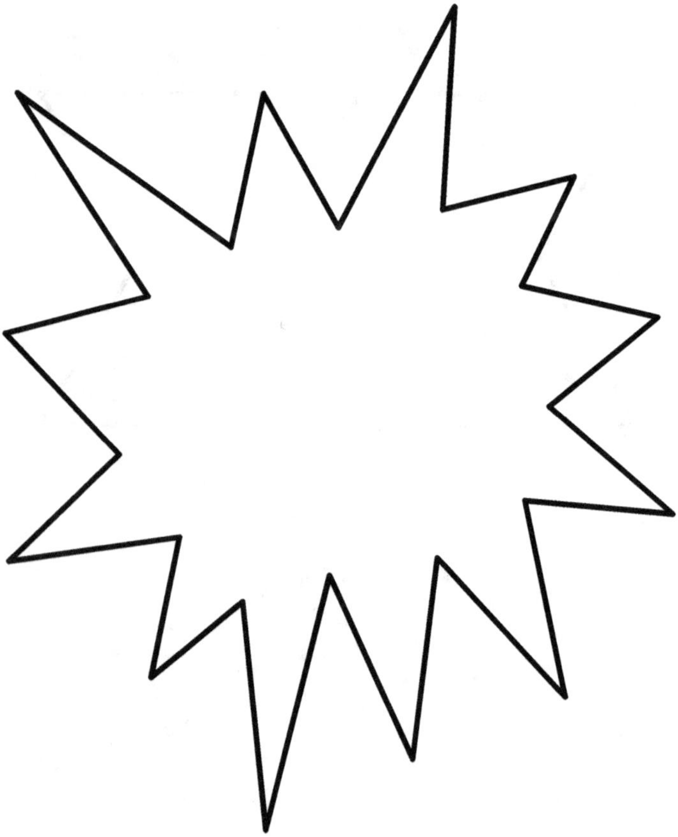

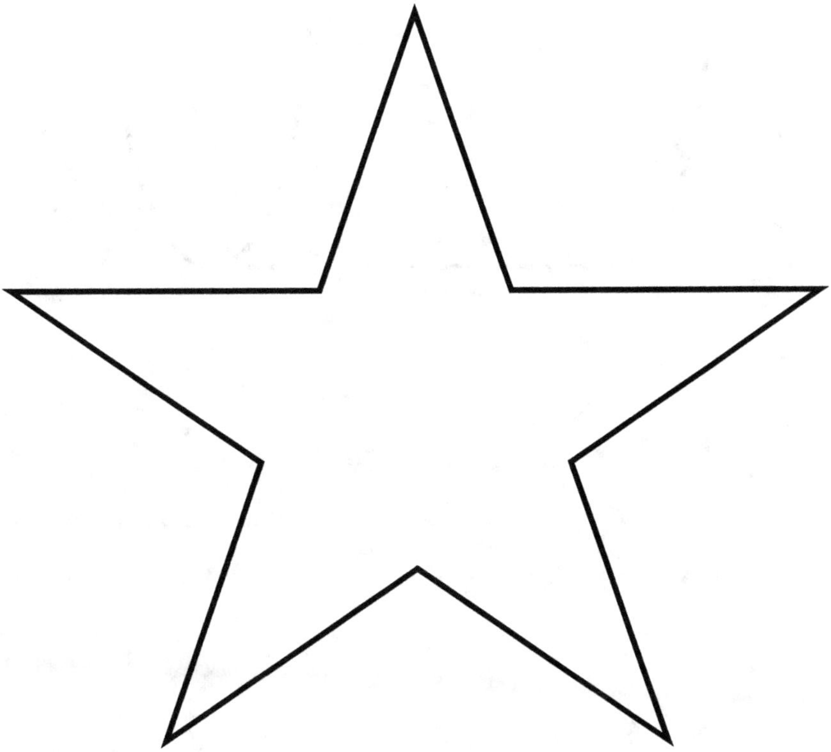

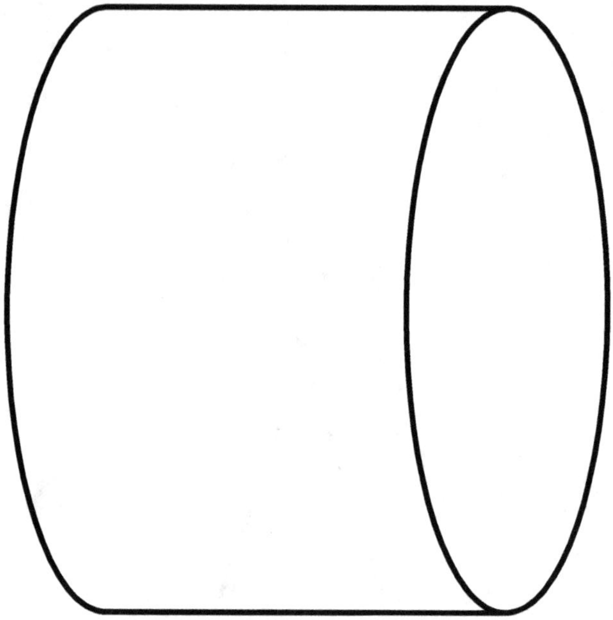

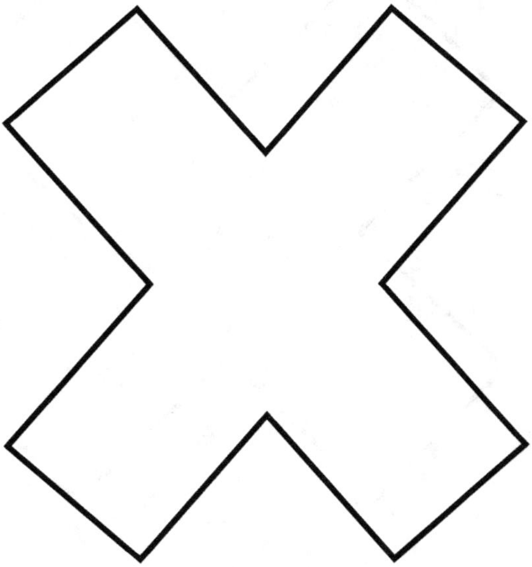

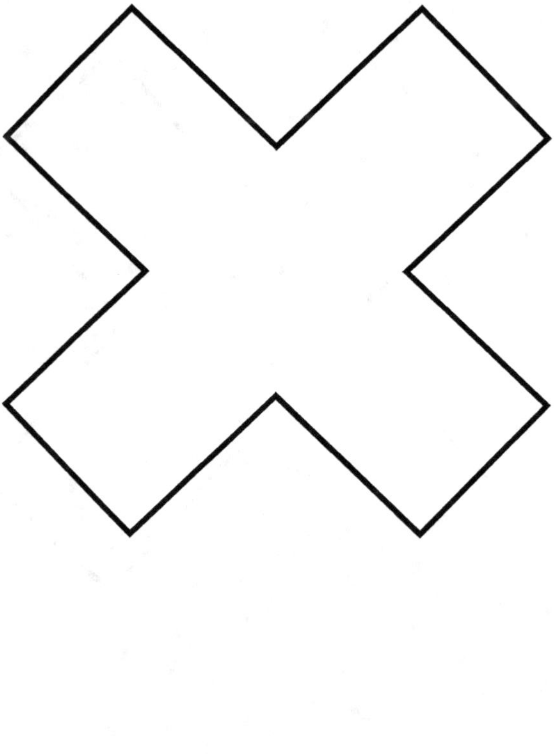

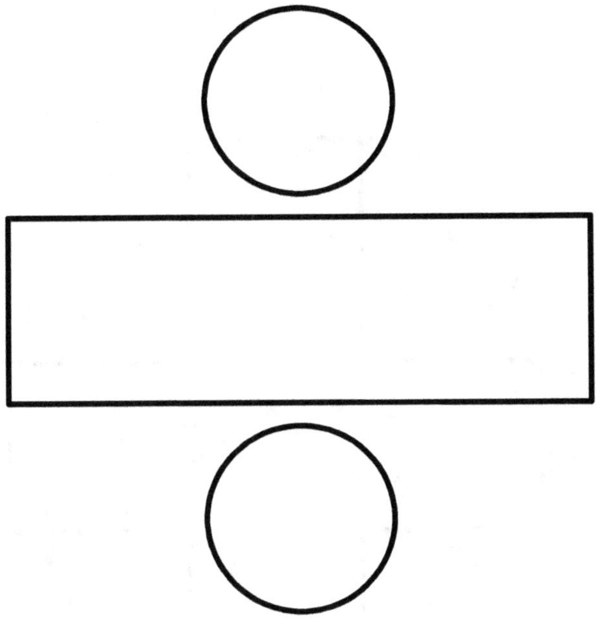

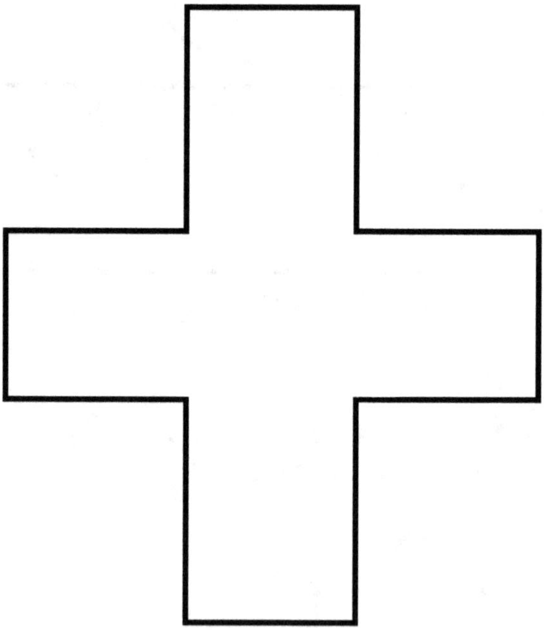

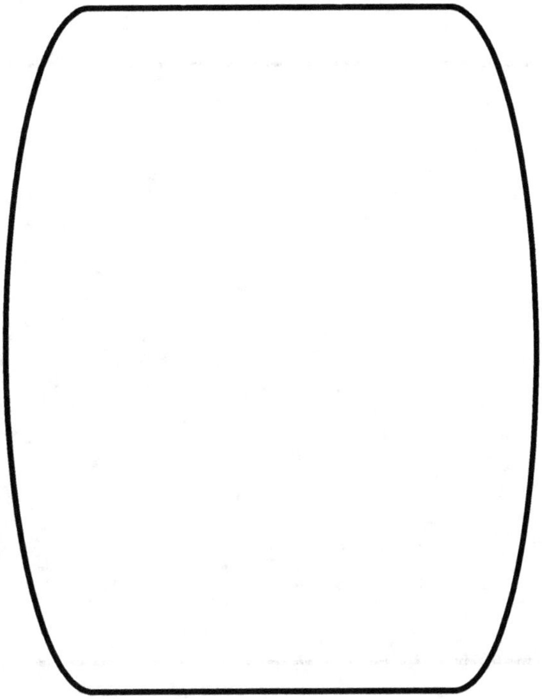

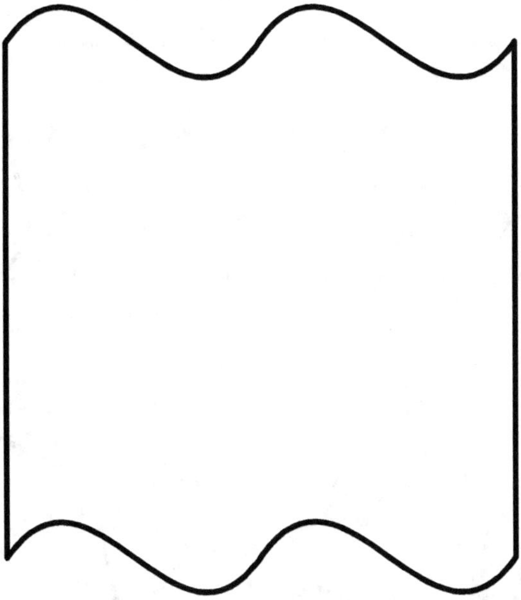

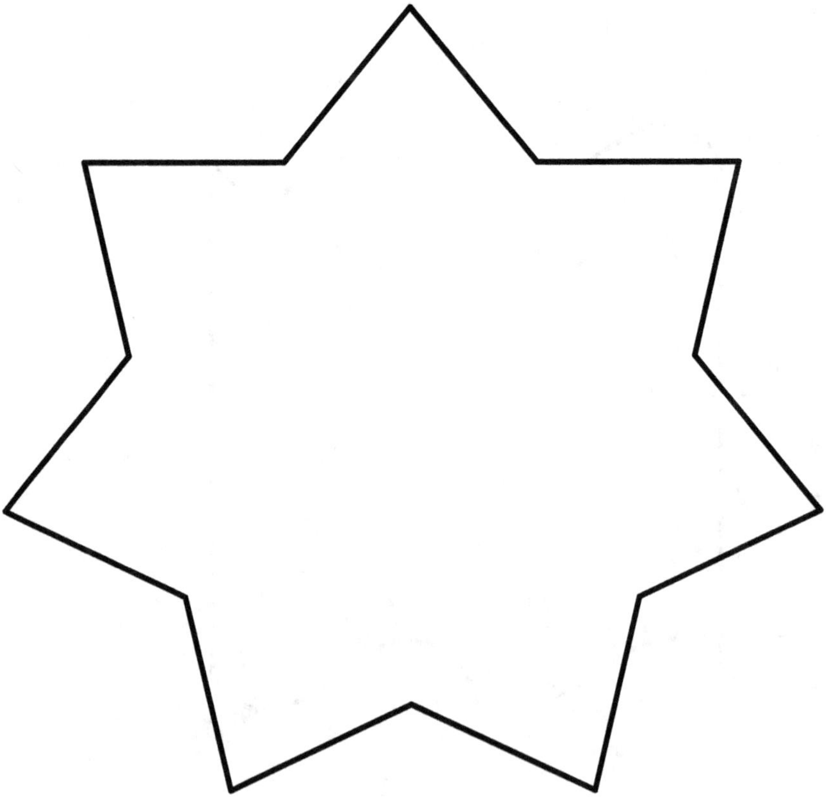

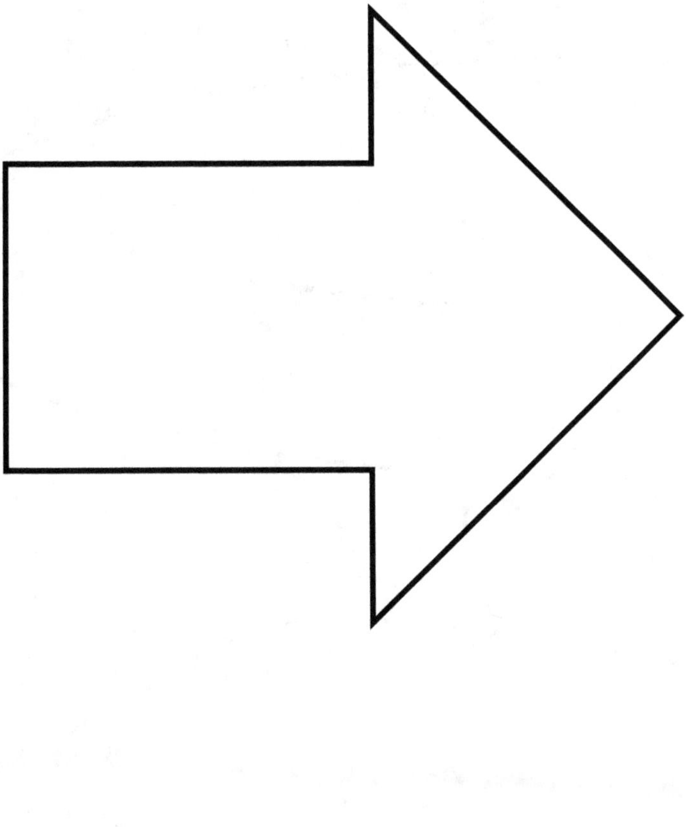

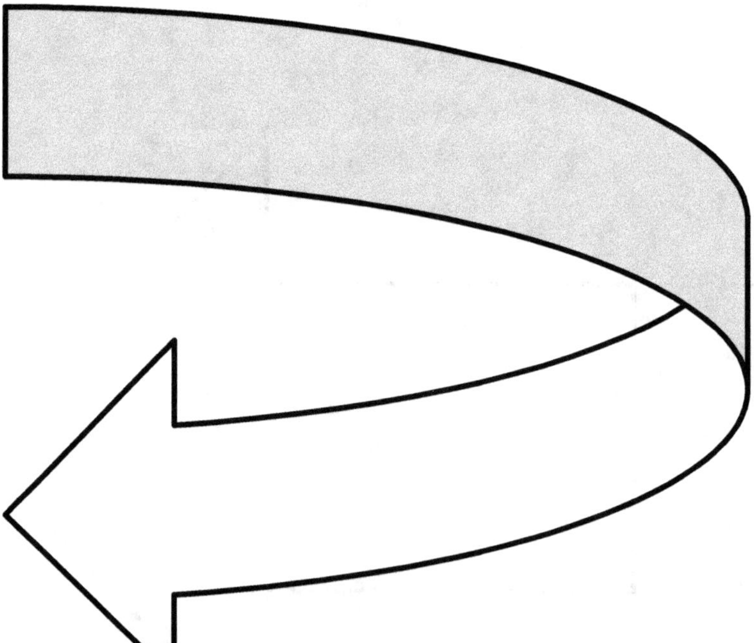

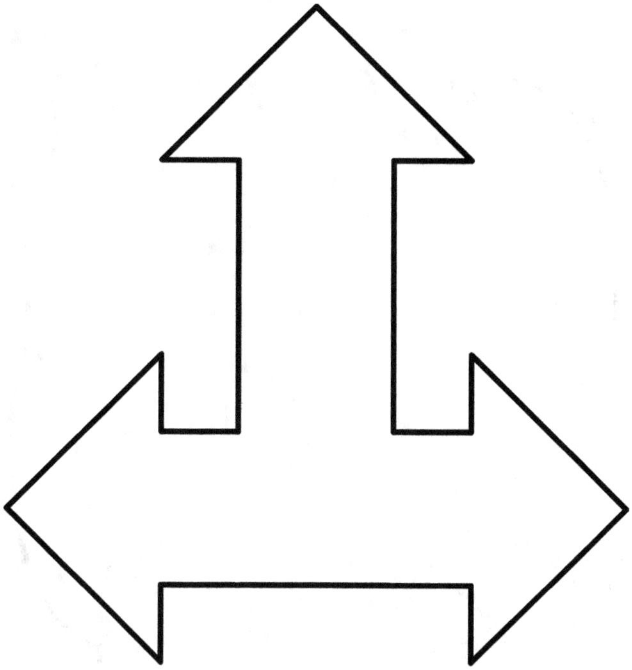

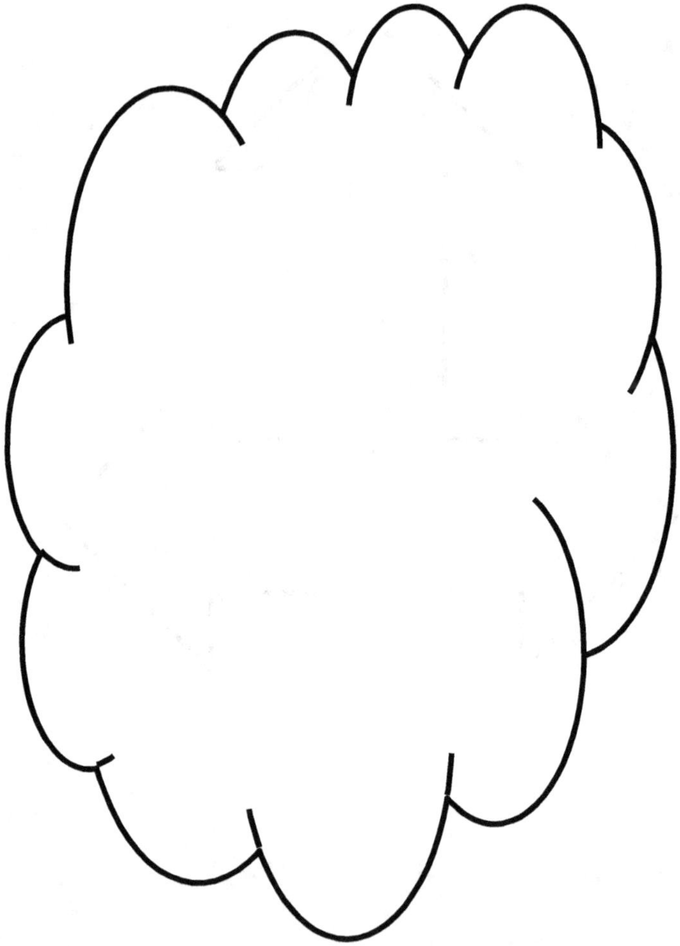

www.ingramcontent.com/pod-product-compliance
Lightning Source LLC
Chambersburg PA
CBHW072259200526
45168CB00016B/2181
* 9 7 8 1 5 1 1 8 2 7 1 1 9 *